MONSTER TRUCKS

TRACY NELSON MAURER

Rourke
Publishing LLC
Vero Beach, Florida 32964

www.rourkepublishing.com

Project Assistance
Ed Newman, AMSOIL INC.
Doc Riley, ESPN2 and Special Events/www.familyevents.com

Also, the author extends appreciation to Kathy Winston, Mike Maurer, and Kendall and Lois M. Nelson.

Photo Credits: All photos © David Huntoon except title page, pp. 8, 9, 16, 42 © K-8 Images; pp. 30, 31, 40, 41 © Ed Newman; p. 38 © Kathy Winston; p. 43 © Virginia Beach Fire Department

Title page: Bigfoot. *One of the first monster trucks built.*

Editor: Frank Sloan

Cover and page design: Nicola Stratford

Notice: The publisher recognizes that some words, model names, and designations mentioned herein are the property of the trademark holder. We use them for identification purposes only. This is not an official publication.

Library of Congress Cataloging-in-Publication Data

Maurer, Tracy, 1965-
  Monster trucks / Tracy Nelson Maurer.
     p. cm. -- (Roaring rides)
Summary: Discusses the history and current popularity of monster trucks, as well as the events at which they race each other and crush junk cars.

Includes bibliographical references and index.
  ISBN 1-58952-749-6 (hardcover)
  1. Monster trucks--Juvenile literature. [1. Monster trucks. 2. Trucks.] I. Title. II. Series: Maurer, Tracy, 1965-   Roaring rides.

TL230.15.M4 2003
796.7--dc21

                                                      2003009766

Printed in the USA

w/w

monster
TABLE OF CONTENTS

Monster trucks thrill crowds with dirt-digging, junker-crushing action.

CHAPTER ONE

BIGGER AND BIGGER

Monster trucks never sneak into an arena. They can't sneak anywhere! These giant trucks stand about 11 feet (3.35 m) tall and measure about 12 feet (3.66 m) wide. Most monster trucks start as a regular pick-up truck or van. They "grow" on top of huge tires and other special parts added by mechanics.

A HUGE SPORT

Monster truck events have grown into a major worldwide attraction. Millions of people watch the hard-charging races and car-crushing action on television. They sit in their clean, comfortable living rooms. That's too bad. They miss the pure excitement that another four million fans enjoy at live events.

In a stadium, the powerful truck engines roar so loudly that the air vibrates—even the grandstand seats shake! Fans love it.

They add their cheers to the wild noise. Indoor and outdoor **venues** across America host competitions almost all year.

Monster truck events are big news now. But before 1979, nobody had ever seen a monster truck.

THE LEGEND OF
Bigfoot

Monster truck fans like to tell the legend of Bigfoot to anyone new to the sport. The tale goes like this:

Back in the 1970s, Bob Chandler loved taking off-road adventures with his 4X4 Ford pick-up truck. Rocks, ruts, and bumps often damaged his prized vehicle. Since he couldn't easily find parts to fix his truck, Bob started his own parts company.

Bob added more and more parts to his truck. It grew bigger. The large truck became a rolling advertisement for his parts company! He named the truck "Bigfoot" because it was his own nickname. Bob's foot was big and heavy on the gas pedal.

Then, in 1979, Bob took Bigfoot to a car show in Denver, Colorado. People flocked to see Bob's monster creation. Bigfoot was a hit!

Bob kept working on Bigfoot. He still drove the truck for fun, too. One day, he drove Bigfoot over a few junked cars—just for fun. The idea took off! About 82,000 fans cheered as Bigfoot crunched junkers at the Silverdome in Pontiac, Michigan, in 1981.

By 1987, Bigfoot and other monster trucks began racing at events. They still crushed cars, competed in pulling contests, and clawed through mud bogs. But freestyle tricks and high-speed races became their main events.

Bigfoot, a Ford truck, crushes the competition. TEAM BIGFOOT now includes 16 trucks and has earned more than seven racing series championships.

THE MONSTER TRUCK HERD

About 200 to 300 monster trucks, each one the size of an elephant, roam the United States now. But elephants seem tame next to these rigs. Every competition truck has a radical name, usually something that sounds mean and strong. A specially shaped body and custom paint-job match the name.

The snake-shaped face and fangs of "Snake Bite" seem ready to spit venom. Many professional monster trucks feature custom designs.

- "Samson" has bulging muscles built into the truck body.

- Red headlights look like evil eyes on "Grave Digger."

- Sharp horns stick out from the "Bulldozer" cab. Fake smoke snorts out the nose on the hood.

- A skull-shaped body makes "Wild Thang" look the creepiest of all.

A few monster truck names sound more normal. "Airborne Ranger" honors American soldiers. Its driver, Joe Cypher, controls the vehicle using hand levers instead of gas or brake pedals. His specially equipped truck was the first one like it in the world to compete. When he's not in the driver's seat, Joe uses a wheelchair. Nothing slows him down!

ROARING FACT:

A custom airbrushed paint job for a monster truck costs from $2,000 to $7,000—each time, crash after crash.

BIGGEST CREATURES ON LAND

	African Bull Elephant	American Monster Truck
Height	About 13 feet (4 m) at shoulder	About 11 feet (3.35 m) at roof
Weight	Up to 8 tons (7,200 kg)	Roughly 4.5 to 5.5 tons (4,080 to 4,990 kg)
Jumps	Can't (wimp)	Well over 100 feet (30.5 m)
Charges	Up to 30 mph (48 kph)	0 to 50 mph (80.5 kph) in less than 3 seconds
Swims	Can dog-paddle	Can float on huge tires
Sprays dust	Uses trunk	Uses tires
Roars	Uses trunk	Uses engine
Consumes	50 gallons (190 l) of water daily	50 gallons (190 l) of methanol per mile
Travels	In herds of up to 100 animals	In convoys of tractor-trailers
Street legal	NO	NO

monster
CHAPTER TWO
BUILT FOR SAFETY

Like Frankenstein, a monster truck is built one at a time by skilled hands. Each hulking machine comes to life after the owners, drivers, and mechanics create a master plan for size, speed, and safety.

Computers help the truck's team to see how to build the vehicle. The U.S. Hot Rod Association (USHRA) makes rules about which parts the owners can use on trucks in competitions. The rules keep the contests fair. They also keep the vehicles and drivers safe.

FILL 'ER UP!

Monster trucks can't fill up at the local gas station. Their engines burn a special methanol racing fuel. It's expensive, too. Methanol costs about $3.50 per gallon, more than double the price of unleaded gasoline.

The owners figure their trucks use about 3 gallons (11.3 liters) for every 250 feet (76.2 m) the vehicle travels—about 50 gallons (189 liters) to the mile. Imagine emptying a gallon bucket of water three times in five seconds or flushing your toilet three times in that five seconds. That's how much fuel disappears in a 250-foot (76.2-m) race.

ROARING FACT:

An engine is measured in cubic inches, or how many cubic inches of liquid would fill up its cylinders. So a 572-cubic-inch engine could hold 572 cubic inches of liquid (roughly 2-1/2 gallons [9.5 liters]).

Each monster truck runs on a huge custom-built engine. The engine delivers the machine's power and speed. Most trucks can run more than 80 miles (128 km) per hour.

The chassis holds the truck together. The engine and the body are attached to its strong steel tubes.

FRAMED JUST RIGHT

The frame, or **chassis**, is the truck's skeleton. It holds the heavy engine about midway, behind the front wheels. The driver sits ahead of the engine.

Computer-aided design (CAD) helps the team decide how to shape the frame's steel tubing. Welders must secure every seam for maximum strength. The team often paints the frame a bright color to show off its neat work. Of course, any truck that **turtles**—flips over on its back—shows off its frame, too.

BALANCED FOR CONTROL

At least one monster truck rolls over at every contest. Still, these huge machines are actually very well balanced. They can even run on just three tires.

Shock absorbers between the wheels and the engine add stability, too. They're part of the **suspension system**—the way the wheels attach to the frame for a smoother ride. Filled with **nitrogen** gas, shock absorbers reduce the bouncing and rocking motion during a ride. They help drivers stay in control longer.

Knowing when to stomp the gas and when to hit the brakes often determine the truck's position at the landing.

BUILT LIGHT

These motorized beasts tip the scales at an easy 5 tons (4,536 kg). That's good for crushing cars, but it's not so good for jumping and racing.

Owners try to cut the truck's weight. Most monster trucks use lightweight fiberglass instead of heavy steel for the bodies. Owners can fix dings and scrapes in fiberglass easily, too. Custom molds to shape the fiberglass can cost more than $20,000 and each body can cost $5,000.

To keep weight off the truck, artists paint fake doors and headlights. The trucks also have no side windows, just webbing. This protects the drivers from broken glass when they crash. Every competition truck must also use special plastic windshields that resist breaking.

Less weight means bigger air on jumps and faster runs on races. The back-end of this monster truck has no floor, making the vehicle lighter.

MONSTER TIRES

A monster truck is nothing without its monster tires. Each tire stands about 66 inches (168 cm) high, almost as tall as a man. The tire measures roughly 45 inches (114 cm) across and weighs 600 pounds (272 kg). The four tires hold enough air to float the truck in water.

Raised ridges in the rubber tires create a deep, hungry tread for better **traction** in dirt. Some drivers whittle the chunky rubber into sharp edges they call "meat hooks" to add traction and lose weight. Of course, they must shave the rubber carefully or they could waste the tire—and money.

A new tire easily costs $2,000. Do the math: four tires times $2,000 equals $8,000. Then add in several spares.

A complete truck costs anywhere from $50,000 to more than $3 million. Now that's some big money!

ROARING FACT:

Strong metal bars (called a roll cage) inside the cab roof protect the driver if the truck rolls over.

Hi-tech gear protects the drivers from head to toe during a crash.

SUITED FOR SAFETY

Competition rules require drivers to wear special racing suits. The layered, lightweight fabric resists fire and gives drivers extra time to safely escape a burning wreck. Most drivers also wear fire-resistant socks and underwear.

Special headgear protects drivers, too. All drivers wear fiberglass helmets made with Kevlar, a material strong enough to stop a bullet. They also wear a fire-resistant headsock under their helmets. Neck collars cushion their heads like stiff pillows. Otherwise, the drivers' heads would rattle and shake during a run.

Drivers can't wear soft sports shoes while they're competing. Instead, they put on hard Kevlar boots that resist fire and bone-breaking blows. Fire-resistant gloves help drivers grip the controls, too.

ROARING FACT:

Most drivers use headphones inside their helmets to hear instructions from their pit crews.

THREE-WAY KILL SYSTEM

If a driver loses control of his vehicle, safety equipment installed inside the monster truck works to protect the driver and other people at an event. The kill system works three ways:

1. The driver can push an emergency stop button to kill the engine.

2. A pull-ring outside the truck at the back allows a track official to quickly stop the motor, if the driver can't.

3. A remote ignition interrupter (RII) installed in each truck lets the judges turn off the motor during an accident. The RII operates like a TV remote control.

A red light glows from the windshield when the kill system is working. Before every race, the drivers must test the RII.

monster
CHAPTER THREE

BEHIND THE WHEEL

Sitting in the cab of a monster truck, the driver looks out the windshield at the fans' faces. The space immediately in front of the vehicle is a "blind spot." The driver cannot see anything—or anyone—there. Some trucks have openings in the cab floors to let the drivers peek at the track.

THE CONTROL CENTER

The cab holds all the controls for handling the monster truck. Many trucks have just one seat. No passengers ride along during an event.

Controlling a monster truck takes **coordination**. One hand holds the steering wheel to direct the front wheels. With the other hand on a lever, the driver shifts gears and steers the rear wheels at the same time. Monster truck drivers spend a lot of time practicing—or gaining "seat time."

SEAT TIME

Many competitive monster truck drivers move up from driving in other motor-sport events.

Generally, drivers must be 25 years old. In addition to a regular driver's license, they must also pass a test for a commercial driver's license. Many drivers lift weights and exercise to stay in good physical shape. Eating right and resting help, too.

Teams that operate several trucks often qualify their drivers. Some teams require a two-year **apprenticeship** before a driver can start practicing alone. With seat time, drivers learn when to gun the engine for a jump. They also learn how to climb up over a stack of junkers to crunch them.

All drivers help maintain their trucks. Most drivers understand mechanics, electronics, or body work.

Some drivers start out driving in "super truck" or "outlaw super truck" events, often held at the same indoor or outdoor venues as the monster truck competitions. Other sideshows at monster truck events include freestyle motocross and quad wars.

LIFE ON THE ROAD

A monster truck must roar like a hurricane when its engine is tuned up right. For a two-hour show, drivers work with their crews all week to check every part. They want to take the next event by storm!

Competing in monster truck events keeps drivers away from home most of the year. The events normally fall on weekends.

During the weekdays, drivers travel with their trucks to the next city on the competition tour. Sometimes they even drive the semi-trucks that haul their huge vehicles. The 18-wheelers serve as garages, too, carrying spare parts and tools for the team.

Monster trucks cannot legally travel on highways. The 18-wheelers that haul them become garages for each event. The team packs the trailer with spare parts and tools.

MONSTER
CHAPTER FOUR
READY TO RUMBLE

Monster trucks started out in the 1980s crushing junkers for sideshows at other motorsport events. **Truck pulls** tested the strength of monster trucks as they tugged away at insanely heavy objects—semi-tractors, trains, buses, or whatever the show promoters could find. A steady driver could also earn trophies and a few bucks at mud-bogging contests for plowing a truck the farthest through a trough of muck.

By the 1990s, the real fun started. Racing and trick competitions became the main events.

SANCTIONED EXCITEMENT

Now monster truck competitions award points to winners at **sanctioned** events. The truck with the most points at the end of the season is the grand champion. The U.S. Hot Rod Association sanctions monster truck competitions, such as the Thunder Nationals, Thunder Drags, Rolling Thunder, Penda Point Series, and the Monster Jam.

Most monster truck events feature head-to-head races and freestyle trick competitions at indoor or outdoor venues. Some use only concrete tracks, while others use dirt. In the Thunder Nationals, the trucks leap onto the junkers *without* ramps!

White and colored paint on the dirt shows the two racing lanes and marks off safety zones for officials in this J-course.

BEHIND THE SCENES

Long before the fans take their seats, a crew works quickly to prepare the stadium or arena. If it's a dirt track, earthmovers haul in tons of sand and gravel. Smaller machines push the dirt into place. Workers pack it down for a hard surface. Jumps, ramps, and **obstacles** take shape.

Workers remove gas tanks, batteries, and glass from a collection of junkers. They paint the cars, buses, or other vehicles bright colors, often yellow or red. They haul the junkers into position.

Pit crews put the finishing touches on the trucks. They wash and polish them. Even the black rubber tires shine.

Just before the big event, a pit party lets the fans meet the drivers. Many fans ask for autographs or photographs. The drivers appreciate their fans, especially the kids.

REVVED TO RACE

Just before the racing begins, the drivers walk the track. The judges also remind the drivers of the rules. All of the drivers test their RII kill systems one last time, too.

To kick off each show, the competing monster trucks rumble around the arena. The drivers rev their engines and spin up dirt.

Then the first two racers bring their monster trucks to the starting line. A thumbs-up gesture from each driver means they're ready to race. At the green flag, they take off. Depending on the event, the track may have jumps, ramps, and obstacles. It may be a straight course or shaped like a J.

A monster truck race lasts about five seconds. The loser is done for the day. The winner moves on to the next heat, until only two racers remain. The final race determines who earns the racing points for that event.

Crunching cars slows down a monster truck. The driver tries to fly through the air as far as possible to gain speed. The steering wheel works only when the tires grip solid ground, however. Controlling the landing is a big part of winning.

TRICK TIME

Many drivers love to race, but they really show their skills during the freestyle part of an event. Each truck takes center stage for 90 seconds. The drivers pop wheelies, spit roostertails of dirt, and mash junked cars. A monster truck show chews through about 25 vehicles at each city.

Sometimes the trucks whip around in circles, making "donuts" in the track. Thick plumes of smoke stream from the tires, too.

They try for big air, soaring as high as 30 feet (9.1 m) off jumps. Monster trucks with bad landings usually need a rescue from a monster tow-truck. A few trucks finish under their own power.

Freestyle events may be judged by other motorsport professionals or by an applause meter. After the freestyle time is up, the audience cheers for their favorite performers. The loudest applause from the crowd decides the winner.

The strong suspension system in a monster truck cushions the hard landings.

CLEAN-UP CREW

Where do the junkers go after the show? After the monster trucks tuck into their big 18-wheelers, a special tractor-trailer pulls into the arena for its load of crushed junkers. Forklifts place the **carnage** on the trailer. The truck takes it to a junkyard where the steel is recycled into new cars.

Mounds of dirt become the ramps for a monster truck track. After the event, crews quickly haul away the extra dirt and flattened junkers.

DRIVER CLOSE-UP:
KATHY WINSTON
TEAM SoBE

Bryan and Kathy Winston seem like typical nice neighbors with a nice family of five kids. But Kathy's got a wild streak in her! In 1994, she started racing Super Trucks—powerful pick-up trucks.

One day, Kathy tried driving a friend's monster truck. She was hooked. A winner in her rookie year, Kathy drove "Inferno" in 2002. She moved into a new monster truck with Team SoBe in 2003. Watch for her to turn up the heat!

CURRENT MAKE/MODEL: All-new Chevrolet S-10

SPECIAL FEATURES: State-of-the-art components, including 2-stage shock system and $45,000 motor; cab adjusted to Kathy's petite 5'3" (1.6m) size

CREW CHIEF: Husband Bryan Winston (now driving Kathy's old truck, "Inferno")

BIRTHDAY: February 28, 1961

RESIDENCE: North Benton, Ohio

COMPETING SINCE: 2002 (age 40)

OTHER PROFESSIONS: Paralegal, mom

CAREER HIGHLIGHTS: Won wheelie, freestyle, and racing events in Evansville, Indiana, during her rookie year; scored a perfect 30 points in freestyle at Providence, Rhode Island, in 2003; one of 16 drivers to compete at the USHRA Monster Jam World Finals in Las Vegas in 2003

HOBBIES: Flying, skydiving, motorcycling, boating, fishing, hunting, and shooting

monster
CHAPTER FIVE

More 4x4 Excitement

Today's monster trucks use tiny onboard computers to monitor performance. New truck parts made with carbon-fiber, magnesium, or titanium materials help the teams build lighter and stronger vehicles. With each new development, the trucks push the limits of the sport to greater heights.

BIGGER, FARTHER, FASTER

Every year, monster truck drivers try to set new world records for their sport.

* One of the Bigfoot trucks runs on 10-foot (3.04-m) tires and stands about 25 feet (7.62 m) tall, the highest so far.

* In 1999, Dan Runte cleared a 14-foot (4.26-m) burning jet in Bigfoot #14, with about 10 feet (3.04 m) to spare. He set a new long-jump record of 202 feet (61.5 m).

- In 1996, Fred Shafer—one of the monster truck drivers with the most wins ever—set the fastest competing time on a 250-foot (76.2-m) track. His truck, Bear Foot, finished in just 4.59 seconds.

Monster truck drivers push their vehicles to jump farther, race faster, and perform better at every event.

MINI MONSTERS

Monster truck fans can't get enough of their motorsport! When they can't watch the trucks on TV or see a live race, some people "drive" their own radio-controlled (RC), miniature monster trucks.

Just like the real trucks, the miniatures require careful planning and building. Hobby stores sell kits, but most owners buy special parts to create unique machines. RC monster trucks pull all kinds of stunts like their big-boy cousins. Rallies with prizes and trophies attract competitors of all ages.

Video games with monster truck characters have become popular, too. Everywhere, people are thinking big—very BIG!

Radio-controlled monster trucks perform stunts just like the big rigs.

Some monster trucks don't play around. This "Big Foot" works for the Virginia Beach Fire Department.

LIBRARY LAUNCH

To learn more about monster trucks, take a spin through the local library. Many books and magazines cover this popular motorsport. Several well-maintained Web sites track the competitions, too.

Of course, nothing beats a seat at a live event!

Monster truck events across America and around the globe deliver non-stop excitement!

Further Reading

Monster Jam: The Amazing Guide by James Buckley, Jr.
  Dorling Kindersley, 2001.

Monster Trucks by Kristin L. Nelson.
   Lerner Publishing Group, 2003.

Monster Trucks by Craig Robert and Robert Carey.
  Random House Children's Books, 2001.

Web Sites

http://www.4wheeloffroad.com
Petersen's 4Wheel & Off-Road Magazine

http://www.familyevents.com
Special Events promotional information

http://www.fourwheeler.com
Four Wheeler Magazine

http://www.MonsterTruckRacing.com
Online monster truck resource

http://www.monstertrucks.net
Online monster truck resource

http://www.rangermotorsports.com/
Airborne Ranger Motorsports

http://www.truckworld.com
Online monster truck resource

http://www.ushra.com
United States Hot Rod Association

Glossary

apprenticeship (ah PREN tiss ship) — a program or contract that hires a less experienced person to learn and practice while working with a more skilled employer

carnage (KAR nij) — what is left behind after a battle

chassis (CHASS ee) — the frame that supports the body of a vehicle

coordination (koh or din AY shun) — skillful body movement; moving in harmony

nitrogen (NIH trah jen) — a colorless, odorless gas

obstacles (OB stah kullz) — things that stand in the way or block a path

sanction (SANGK shun) — to approve or to allow; to make rules

suspension system (sah SPEN shun SISS tihm) — in vehicles, the system of shock absorbers, springs, and other parts between the wheel and chassis designed to create a smooth ride and better control

traction (TRAK shun) — sticking or gripping to a surface

truck pulls (TRUK PULZ) — a contest for trucks to test how much weight the vehicles can pull

turtle (TUR tihl) — in motor sports, to crash and land so that the vehicle is flipped upside down

venues (VEN yooz) — places that host concerts, contests, and other events, usually with viewing areas to see the action

Index

About The Author

Tracy Nelson Maurer specializes in nonfiction and business writing. Her most recently published children's books include the RadSports series, also from Rourke Publishing LLC. Tracy lives with her husband Mike and two children near Minneapolis, Minnesota.